THE EVOLUTION OF MARRIAGE

THE EVOLUTION OF MARRIAGE

Relationships Through the Ages

AVERY NIGHTINGALE

QuantumQuill Press

CONTENTS

CHAPTER 1

Introduction

Examining the history of relationships can contribute to our understanding of the character of modern relationships, their social context, and purpose. Our own relationships are scrutinized here, in the context of earlier understandings, to consider the pressures to which they are subjected and the positions taken up as a consequence. Only by understanding something of the history of human relationships can we see them for what they really are. Because of the essential religious significance of marriage in the medieval period, an understanding of how religious authorities saw it is particularly important. Their understanding does not present a general character of human relationships, but it does give a particularly interesting account of what people were encouraged to believe was the purpose and character of marriage. The majority of marriages are, and have always been, for nonreligious reasons; only those that were contracted not to be consummated and that were therefore liable to be annulled on the request of one or both parties were generally weddings in a religious, i.e. Christian, sense.

At the heart of every human society lies the family. In today's western culture, relationships are often seen solely as matters of personal choice, the benefits of which are expected to be self-evident to those who decide to enter into them. The idea of two people getting married is generally considered a happy and socially acceptable one. However, individual experience tells us that the relationship between persons is seldom always perfect; indeed, it can be very difficult. Moreover, history suggests that the relationship between the two sexes has always been complex, and frequently much more stressed than modern western eyes might care to suppose. As with any complex and living institution, the shape and purpose of relationships changes over time - evolving, sometimes unexpectedly, to accommodate contemporary pressures and society's greater understanding of itself. Traditional systems become challenged as contemporary pressures reshape the structure of the connections between humans.

CHAPTER 2

Prehistoric Relationships

Humans at that time had wider hips than today, and their offspring's heads were large. This combination forced them to be born prematurely and stay near their mothers for much of the time. When they stood up on two legs to carry food from one base to the other, they used their front members to carry their offspring and their tasks. To free themselves of the children and be more efficient carriers, they invented a tie fashioned of a strip of animal skin that went around the front member. The scientists who studied the archaeological sites where those first ties were discovered believe they were used to carry children, which freed the wearers' hands. Called Papoose Front Packs, they had two branches, like a Y, and a large knot at the lower part of the Y, presumably to reinforce the security of the pack. Indeed, both visual images and scientific evidence suggest that mothers wore them routinely.

There were no same-sex couples on Earth when Homo sapiens evolved in Africa, around 200,000 years ago. About 50,000 years later, however, there was a kind of marriage in place between them. They crafted stone tools and tamed fire. An animal species that had always mated in the open, unprotected from predators, started to live in small groups in the darkness of caves. Researchers have recently found some 4,000 bone fragments, predominantly of children, that had been littered inside a cave believed to be among the first human sites. Child burials were odd at a time when bodies were usually abandoned outdoors or, at most, around settlement locations, to be gnawed on by animals, even those that belonged to the same genus as Homo sapiens (the Neanderthals).

CHAPTER 3

Ancient Civilizations and Marriage

To ameliorate the situation, many men were not married to one woman, but were instead married to his wife's sister. Therefore, when one wife passed away, his other wife could be promoted to the status of wife and nothing would change. The roles of men and women in ancient civilizations were very different than they are today. The woman was only seen as property and had almost no rights whatsoever. The men were the backbone of society and could do virtually anything they wanted. In the play, Oedipus the King, the heroine says "'Then I will walk my path to the very end,'" this is a clear quote that shows the control of men in societies where there were no rights for women. Despite such challenging relationships, it is natural for societal norms to change and today, although men still have some of the upper hand, women have come a very long way since then and the future can only continue to grow and prosper.

Looking back in history, it is easy to see evidence that marriage was very different in ancient civilizations. In those societies, marriage was always arranged or common law. There was no such thing as "marriage for love." A decision to marry was not up to the individual. Rather, the parents would unite the two and there was no consent from either party. Women had no control over the male relatives; they were always under the control of a man. This period was known as proprietary marriage. There are several views as to how women were subjected to the control of the man, but we have found no custom where a wife was under the power of anyone but her husband. With that said, men went into the marriage without knowing who their wife was and therefore did not know if they would be compatible.

CHAPTER 4

Marriage in Medieval Times

During the medieval times, 'agape', 'eros', and interests were seen as causes for different types of marriages. Marriages made out of agape consisted of two people who were of service to the church and community, while eros marriages were based upon physical desire, and interests marriages included families in need of protection, love, or money. The Church was selective about whom to marry based on the different criteria, so not all marriages were formed for true love and beauty. While agape marriages were rare, the church certainly encouraged them as it allowed couples to express their feelings, which would later turn into the true Christian love as time passed. When eros marriages were developed, many people would empathize with this passionate and desire-filled love, as the feelings involved with this formed natural love within the couple. This alone wasn't a big deal, as individual feelings according to Augustine were of no personal importance to the church. However, when the couple sealed the bond by taking up the vows, the Christian love was established.

The institution of marriage was developed in the medieval times when people were encouraged to join in matrimony for reasons like creating alliances, building kingdoms, and protection. The church was seen as an influential and major power, as it had helped in the development of the social standards of marriage. The marriage sacrament, which the church believed to be the only legitimate way to get married, was contingent on mutuality between the two spouses, as this would turn their natural love into a pure Christian form of love. The sacrament thus attempted to bond the couple and to bind the personal feelings with a Christian understanding as well.

CHAPTER 5

Renaissance and Enlightenment Era Marriages

The idea behind much of the property laws was to ward off the fear that a man would die without a son to inherit his family's riches. Daughters, and their husbands, receiving dowries was a way to keep dowry property within the family if sons couldn't be born to carry the family name and provide for one's parents in their old age. Authors Tannahill and Tillyard, who write about marriage in Italy, note that any man of substance had an obligation to marry a girl from an equally important family, enough dowry to allow her to begin a successful marriage in a family of her own. The dowry, of course, needed to be paid not only by the lady love but by all of the family—mother, father, and even other relatives—who would unite in an effort to purchase the most eligible match. In the event that both parties in the marriage were deemed worthy of excessive dowries by their families, the marriage could be set up so that neither party would advance nor would they be at a loss when entering into married life.

Renaissance weddings are known for being grand, especially for families in the upper class. In Italy, people were known for their clannish beliefs, and marriage was seen as an event that brought two families together, both in surname and property. Marriages were generally arranged by family members, and the betrothed themselves had little to do with the union. A dowry typically accompanied the marriage. The dowry wasn't meant solely to show the worth and value of the bride, but also to financially protect her in the event of the untimely death of her husband. It was a little like buying life insurance for a wife. If she outlives her spouse, it was accepted that she would return to her father's house with her dowry. Furthermore, Boccaccio noted that if there were one or two daughters in a family, the eldest was never to be given a very large dowry. Excessive dowries were seen as setting a bad example for a family and discouraging other respectable people from marrying.

CHAPTER 6

Industrial Revolution and Changing Dynamics

Falling in love was declared something to be praised, not taken with caution. Since a marriage sparked by love often led to homes nourished by the ethical management of one's own family, something had shifted for everyone. Better suited than boredom or calculation, love promised that family life could thrive long after the couple's wedding day. Anatole France, a Nobel Prize-winning novelist around the turn of the 20th century, may have celebrated the onset of modern love's middle-class power when he wrote, "We have launched a thousand ships, but only to bring Helen back." The J.R.R. Tolkien of his time, he probably echoes Hector's wistful regret for his doomed fight against Achilles—otherwise war's prize could never teach people virtues reserved for heroes. With her soldiers preoccupied with warring, Helen remained unharmed while "hers is the Argive camp's enticing laughter".

In the past, marriage served a far more cold-hearted purpose: it was the critical factor in whether you led a life of drudgery with little love and much hardship or a life of relative ease with long-term companionship. From a romantic perspective, the history of marriage is a very modern one. Procreation and inheritance often took precedence over comfort, compatibility, or love. As soon-to-be-married aristocrats flocked to churches to unite with their partners of choice, the English poet, philosopher, and courtier Philip Sidney found it disgraceful for men to "bind themselves forever to the society of a woman of whose suiting he now is least assured". Europeans still practiced arranged marriages that almost always made economic, historical, or political sense. Yet centuries later, people across all classes began to choose matrimony for the heart connections it could ensure—instigating the love marriage that has since transformed our way of life more than anything else after the Agricultural Revolution.

CHAPTER 7

Marriage in the Victorian Era

This time period did not differ significantly between classes, as it was believed that women should be well versed in the art of homemaking. When interacting with servants, supervising the running of the house, and seeing to the training and education of the children, even the wealthiest women of the United States were still expected to know how to carry out these duties. As housewives, women were tasked with establishing their family among society as well as teaching responsibility, how to run a home, and other traits daughters would need as wives to carry on the moral duties of motherhood themselves. A woman of this time period not only was confined to her house and family but was not as prominent in the newspaper and journals as she did not partake in the larger society. Her primary role was the governance of the household and supervision of all household staff and items, such as the books, china, and general conduct of completely domestic servants.

Mary Wollstonecraft, an 18th-century writer, wrote of the dangers of an unequal marriage for women throughout history in her book "A Vindication of the Rights of Women". She emphasized how marriage turns women into domestic slaves, and a woman's freedom was determined by the choice she made in choosing a husband. Society in America at the time had not only rules and expectations for wives, but it also fostered the subordinate position of women in the family and raised them to believe this was the proper role. Though the 18th-century emphasized the importance of the husband, women of all classes did continue to assume a traditional role in the home along with responsibilities of wife and mother, both of which were thought to be essential to a peaceful family life. Motherhood and home were vital to society, and women were to be the cornerstone that created the foundation of virtue and religion to be transmitted to their offspring.

CHAPTER 8

20th Century: Changing Roles and Attitudes

The Census Bureau in 1947 identified two "ideal" types of women, namely, the housewife and the career woman. Prospects for a third category of women, the "career-housewife", were considered to be remote. The post-war period furthermore is considered as a brief moment during which American women briefly "returned" to home in order to embrace traditional roles. The Golden Age of the 1950s after when the American economy was booming awarded men and women with relative comfort and prosperity. At the same time, women's magazines such as Redbook emphasized and celebrated women's participation in the world of shopping, cooking and patriotic chit-chat. It was around the 1960s that the role of women became a subject, in a renewed manner, that needed re-evaluation.

The 20th century was a time of enormous change in American life. The invention of the automobile, the growth of suburbs, and massive growth of the population that lived in them led to profound changes in the social structure and interactions of Americans. The United States, already racially and ethnically diverse, saw rising tensions around immigration and the cultural dislocation that it can bring. The relationship of men and women changed dramatically in ways that would have been thought unthinkable prior to World War II. This period can be thought of as between the "traditional" and "modern" periods culturally. Looking at attitudes toward marriage is instructive in understanding the ways in which the marriage relationship has evolved within American society and culture.

CHAPTER 9

Modern Marriage: Challenges and Transformations

Americans place a higher value on emotional satisfaction and intimacy in their partnerships, staying in relationships that deliver open communication and meaningful and practical support while leaving unhealthy or unsatisfying relationships. They are less likely to stay in a connection that lacks intimacy or that has become toxic. Unfortunately, while Americans are increasingly seeking high-quality relationships, they still lack the skills and preparation to navigate the inherent challenges of such an intimate and complex connection. As a result, rough waters can lead to relationship breakdowns or continued, yet unsatisfying, relationships. It is the responsibility of society to recognize and extend the support and education needed to enhance the likelihood of life-long satisfaction and happiness in marital relationships. Given the dramatic technological and workplace transformations that are pushing couples apart and stretching marriages toward a 50-year duration, Americans need to apply high-quality interactions, skills and resources to help individuals create and sustain healthy and satisfying marital relationships.

Today, Americans are redefining the institution of marriage by developing new ways to strengthen and extend its impact, waiting longer to marry, and embracing new living arrangements. They are stretching the boundaries of an institution that formerly excluded many individuals and relationships, demonstrating ways to build lasting commitments that defy old paradigms and creating family structures that expand the concept of family. While work remains to strengthen this and other societal institutions that support enduring relationships, we believe that marriage today is a more rewarding, enjoyable, and successful relationship than ever. Compared to past decades, people now marry later and have more freedom to select and peer evaluate their partners from a larger pool of possible spouses. As a result, marriages are increasingly harmonious, and people have more mutually satisfying relationships with their romantic partners than in the past.

CHAPTER 10

The Future of Marriage

"We've seen a remarkable amount of unchanging paired together with a remarkable amount of changing," says W. Bradford Wilcox, a professor of sociology at UVA. If you look internationally, marriage itself is changing the world over in ways such as an incredibly dramatic drop in the rate of marriage in Korea. Internally, within the United States, many different groups have seen many different types of marriage trends. About one in ten college-educated women in the age group of 35 to 39 are divorced, while for those without a college degree it's about the same rate for the never-married. When you look at the opposite group in the same class, it's clear that there's a rapid erosion of differentials: it's not a great trend for the college educated. In many non-Western societies, people form groups of cohabitating domestic structures, and that's what social life is. Throughout history, marriage has been all types of different things; either a group of sexually available and dependent female slaves, a coverture - the merger of two legal entities as husband and wife - a sex desert to which there were sparse visits from a center of physical beauty, an inquiring lover, a guarantee for the political stability of the state and children, or a public announcement made by two people. Or three. Or more. More recently, for any two people at any time in all of America, even someone younger than fifty, marriage has gone through many bizarre changes.

Despite these high-profile incidents, there's evidence that marriage is on the rise - in some cases, quite dramatic. Sociologists at Bowling Green State University have been studying census data since the early 80s and have turned some of the national curiosity around the apparent decline in marriage. "Not only is it not disappearing," says researcher Wendy Manning, "but it's actually increasing." Even at the college-education level, Manning believes marriage has bottomed out and is also on the rise. And in the wake of a worldwide recession, the trend toward marriage equality - a protracted legal struggle - suggests that each side is fighting for the benefits of formalized, contracted kinship. That is, the married, at least on one level, are fighting for their right not to join the ranks of the simply cohabitating. Overall, humankind seems to be heading relentlessly toward a concept, a definition of what it is to be married.

Milton Keynes UK
Ingram Content Group UK Ltd.
UKHW040329031224
452051UK00011B/318

9 798330 618040